Loving Moments

Loving Moments

A TREASURY OF ROMANTIC WRITINGS

Hallmark Editions

Selected by Aileene Herrbach Neighbors.

The publisher wishes to thank those who have given their kind permission to reprint material included in this book. Every effort has been made to give proper acknowledgments. Any omissions or errors are deeply regretted, and the publisher, upon notification, will be pleased to make necessary corrections in subsequent editions.

Acknowledgments: "Love does not consist..." from *Wind, Sand and Stars* by Antoine de Saint-Exupéry. Copyright, 1939, by Antoine de Saint-Exupéry, copyright, 1967, by Lewis Galantiere. Reprinted by permission of Harcourt Brace Jovanovich, Inc. and William Heinemann, Ltd. "Love Is a Constant Thing" from *Poems of Inspiration and Courage* by Grace Noll Crowell. Copyright 1936 by Harper & Row, Publishers, Inc.; renewed 1964 by Grace Noll Crowell. Reprinted by permission of the publisher. "The Basic Passion" from *Three to Get Married* by Fulton J. Sheen. Copyright 1951 by Fulton J. Sheen. Reprinted by permission of Hawthorn Books, Inc. "Fittingly" by Marlene K. Close. ⓒ1975 Downe Publishing, Inc. Reprinted by permission of *Ladies' Home Journal* and the author. "A Song of Love" by Jessyca Russell Gaver. ⓒ1975 Downe Publishing, Inc. Reprinted by permission of *Ladies' Home Journal* and the author. "Seasonings" by Jean Herrod. ⓒ1973 Downe Publishing, Inc. Reprinted by permission of *Ladies' Home Journal* and the author. "Song" reprinted with permission of Macmillan Publishing Co., Inc. from *Collected Poems* by Sara Teasdale. Copyright 1911 by Sara Teasdale. Copyright 1922 by Macmillan Publishing Co., Inc. Excerpt from *All the Love in the World* by Mary Parrish. Copyright 1961 by Mary Parrish, reprinted by permission of Harold Matson Co., Inc. "Love Song" by William Carlos Williams from *Collected Earlier Poems.* Copyright 1938 by New Directions Publishing Corporation. Reprinted by permission of New Directions Publishing Corporation. "This is the miracle..." reprinted from *Letters of Rainer Maria Rilke, 1892-1910*, translated by Jane Bannard Greene and M. D. Herter Norton. By permission of W. W. Norton & Company, Inc. Copyright 1945 by W. W. Norton & Company, Inc. Copyright renewed 1972 by M. D. Herter Norton. "The Law of Love" from *Hope for Man* by Joshua Loth Liebman. Copyright ⓒ1966 by Fan Loth Liebman. Reprinted by permission of the publisher, Simon & Schuster, Inc. "Together we have faced..." and "Down Life's Highway" by Emily Carey Alleman. Copyright 1957 by Emily Carey Alleman. Reprinted by arrangement. "Hour of Night" by Esther York Burkholder. Copyright 1953 by Esther York Burkholder. Reprinted by arrangement. "To My Love" by Maureen Cannon from *Modern Bride*. Copyright ⓒ1970 by Maureen Cannon. Reprinted by arrangement. "Recompense" by Katherine Edelman. Copyright 1954 by Katherine Edelman. Reprinted by arrangement. "Commuters' Special" by Florence B. Jacobs. ⓒ1959 by Florence B. Jacobs. Reprinted by arrangement. "Words for an Autumn Heart" by Gladys McKee. From *Extension* Magazine, Chicago, Illinois. Reprinted by arrangement. "My Dream" from *Close to the Heart* by Helen Lowrie Marshall. Copyright ⓒ1958 by Helen Lowrie Marshall. Reprinted by arrangement. "January Love Letter" by Frances Higginson Savage. Reprinted by permission of Frances Higginson Savage and *The Lyric*. "New Forever" by Clara Aiken Speer. Copyright 1954 Curtis Publishing Company. Reprinted by arrangement. Excerpt from *Autumn Love Song* by Jesse Stuart. ⓒ1971 by Hallmark Cards, Inc. Reprinted by arrangement.

TO MY LOVE

Our days are like a string of beads,
Each small perfection
Enlarged and magnified somehow
By the reflection
Of each on each.

Maureen Cannon

DOWN LIFE'S HIGHWAY

Hand in hand, together,
   Traveling life's highway;
We find the journey pleasant,
   Sharing day by day.

Sharing the sweet and the bitter,
   Sharing the pleasure and pain,
We take the sun with the shadow,
   Laugh at the silver rain.

Laugh at the storms and brave them,
   Seeking to understand;
We find the fruit of life sweeter,
   Traveling hand in hand.

Emily Carey Alleman

SEASONS OF LOVE

Spring
I love you in the springtime
When the sky is clear and blue
And all the days are lovelier
Because they're spent with you.

Summer
I love you in the summer,
Through each carefree, sunny day,
With a love that goes much deeper
Than words could ever say.

Autumn
I love you in the autumn
When the leaves are red and gold
And we harvest all the happiness
Two loving hearts can hold.

Winter
I love you in the wintertime
When frost is in the air
And the world becomes
          a wonderland
Of happiness to share.

Rebecca Thomas Shaw

6

FITTINGLY

The silver splendor of the stars,
The pale orbs of Sun and Moon,
Flowers and trees in myriad hues
Which Nature's hand has deftly strewn;
The mysteries of Life and Death,
Precious gems and their rarity,
The Seven Wonders of the World,
And all the beauty of the sea.
Your name, my love, I list with these,
My cheeks are warm, my heart aglow,
Yes, I must sing your praises here,
Because it seems so apropos.

Marlene K. Close

The rose speaks of love
Silently, in a language
Known only
to the heart.

Dean Walley

TREASURED MOMENTS

Somebody's always in my mind
Like a beautiful thought, all silver lined,
When I'm walking somewhere
       or driving through town
Or strolling where friendly stars look down.

Somebody's always in my mind
Like an old sweet song, the lasting kind,
And it's easy to see why I can't forget,
For heaven began when first we met.

Mary Dawson Hughes

The sea has its pearls,
     The heaven its stars,
But my heart, my heart,
     My heart has its love.

Heinrich Heine

8

WHAT IS A SWEETHEART?

A sweetheart is the someone
You could write a book about,
The one you love to be with
And you hate to be without.

A sweetheart is a knowing look,
A hand within your own,
The voice you always want to hear
When you pick up the phone.

A sweetheart understands your moods
And laughs at things you say
Or sees you when you're at your worst
But loves you anyway.

A sweetheart is the one you kiss
And make up with again
When there's a little difference
Of opinion now and then.

A sweetheart is the someone
That you're always thinking of,
And the very special reason
Why you know that you're in love.

Katherine Nelson Davis

A WOMAN'S HEART

A woman's heart is a delicate thing,
Like a gossamer thread
      or a butterfly's wing;
Easily broken, quick to heal,
Readily given, hard to steal.
Bountiful riches, wonderful bliss
Has he who holds a treasure like this.
Graciously given by Heaven above,
A woman's heart and a woman's love.

Reginald Holmes

MY QUIET PLACE

The world
    keeps spinning, spinning,
    and the days
    go rushing by,
    and sometimes
    there is scarcely time
    to stop
    and wonder why...
But, inside me,
    there's a quiet place
    where hope and faith renew,
    where the world, the world
    can't reach me...
That quiet place is you.

Francee Davis

THE MIRACLE OF LOVE

To be loved is to know
happiness and contentment.
To give love is to know
the joy of sharing oneself.
It is through the miracle of love
that we discover the fullness of life.

Hadin Marshall

CHANGE

When we first met, our love was filled
with promises for tomorrow. But we are
wiser now. We fill our love with the joys
of today so our love will not become
a mere memory of yesterday.

Barbara Bartocci

Together we have faced
    life's yesteryears
And in them known
    the beauty of completeness,
Our hearts have felt
    the lash of sorrow's tears
And salvaged sweetness.

Emily Carey Alleman

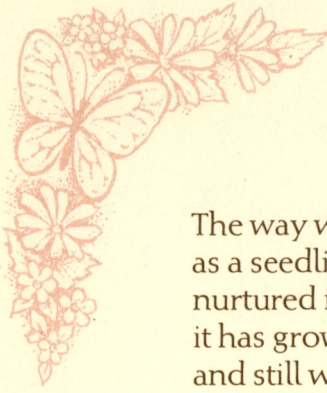

The way we love is a living thing. It started
as a seedling, tender and immature, was
nurtured in the sharing of our lives, until now—
it has grown beyond our wildest imagining—
and still we find new blooms, more
perfect every day.

Heather O'Neal

*Love is the emblem
of eternity: it confounds
all notion of time,
effaces all memory
of a beginning,
all fear
of an end.*

Madame de Staël

WHAT IS LOVE?

Love's no wild, unearthly thing
    rung in with bells
       or brought on a bright dove's wing.

No, love is an everyday affair
    as comfortable as cushions
       on a favorite chair,
    as dear as the old, worn slippers
       one prefers to wear.

Love is an everyday delight
    as simple as smiling,
       and polite,
    as reassuring, pleasant, plain
       as a kiss good-night.

Love is an ordinary thing.

Yet, love's familiar patterns
    seem to bring
       a dove-bright joy to every day.

Because of love, somehow,
    bells ring!

Barbara Kunz Loots

15

SOMETHING CALLED LOVE

When there's someone,
    one someone,
  who makes your days brighter,
  makes your joys greater,
  makes your heart lighter,
Someone,
    one someone,
  you want so to share with,
  do everything with,
  go everywhere with,
Someone,
    one someone,
  you want to live for—
  you have that something
  called love.

Karen Ravn

MY DREAM

When first I dreamed
    of how our love would be,
So shallow was my dream,
    how could I see
The whole great, matchless depth
    of ripened love?
Can earthbound hearts
    envision Heaven above?

When first we two
    were sweethearts, you and I,
I did not dream how swift
    the time would fly;
How every perfect day would be,
    when gone,
The prelude to a
    still more perfect dawn.

In all my dreams
    I never knew the power
That love could have
    to sweeten every hour;
The quiet joy
    I find in your caress,
The sweet content
    of our togetherness....

The dream was just a glimpse
God gave to me,
One fleeting glimpse
of sweet reality.

Helen Lowrie Marshall

I LOVE YOU TRULY

I love you truly, truly dear,
Life with its sunshine,
life with its tears,
Fades into dusk when I know
you are near, dear,
For I love you truly, truly dear.

Carrie Jacobs-Bond

*Love has the power
to alter the hour...
to shape our destiny.*

Charles Morgan

THE GIFT OF LOVE

Love is a gift that cannot be demanded,
A blessing that comes from the heart.
And those who are sharing it
        find their thoughts turning
To heaven, where love had its start.
Love is a pledge that will never be broken,
A trust that will ever be true,
And when it is sent from an unselfish heart,
It's returned in full measure to you!

Barbara Plumb

*I wear your love
        and they say it shows
Like a dewdrop
        glistening on a rose.*

Nancy Baker Smith

FOREVER, LOVE

I shall love you today and tomorrow,
my love...And in all the tomorrows
there are...I shall love you as long as
there lingers a song...And the sky has
a single star...In the spring when
the wind is a gentle breeze...And the
rain and the roses are here...In the
summery days when the friendly rays...
Of the golden sun appear...In the lonely
lap of the autumn months...Where the
beautiful leaves must fall...And again
in the night when the fields are white...
In the folds of their wintry shawl...
I shall love you while ever a mountain
stands...And the waves of the ocean
pass...And until the sands of the
farthest lands...Have run through the
hour-glass...I shall love you as much
as my heart can love...Wherever,
my love, you are...I shall love you
as long as there lingers a song...And
the sky has a single star.

James J. Metcalfe

A SONG OF LOVE

There's such a wide, wide world
Out there
I guess that's nothing new
Except the fact there's no one else
I could ever love but you...

Of course, the world is occupied
By many more, I know
But I can only think of one
Who makes me feel this glow...

If all of this sounds like a song
Then sing in harmony...
I love you darling, and you are
This whole wide world
To me.

Jessyca Russell Gaver

THANK YOU FOR YOUR LOVE

Thank you for—
> *Yesterday*
>> When our lifetime together
>> was only beginning,
>>> and I was just starting to know
>> Your everyday habits,
>> your kind, gentle ways
>>> and the thoughtfulness
>>> you always show,
>
> *Today*
>> When you're here to give me
>> the wonderful comfort
>>> of knowing you listen and care,
>> And we grow ever closer
>> in so many ways,
>>> making memories
>>> to cherish and share,
>
> *Always*
>> As we face each tomorrow
>> so gladly together
>>> with dreams we can watch
>>> coming true,
>> And I'll find that whatever
>> the future may hold
>>> will be precious
>>> because there is you.

Karen Ravn

24

RECOMPENSE

This is the recompense for all—
This sitting by the fire at evening,
The lamps turned low,
The long day over.
Through time and the passing of days
The heart will treasure most
These moments of quiet companionship,
Making no demand for speech,
Or for meeting of hands and lips;
The silence between
An unworded song,
Heartwarming, reassuring
As the singing flame upon the hearth.

Katherine Edelman

*There is nothing sweeter
    than love's memory...
unless it is
    love's dream.*

Margaret Benton

LOVE SONG

Sweep the house clean,
hang fresh curtains
in the windows,
put on a new dress
and come with me!
The elm is scattering
its little loaves
of sweet smells
from a white sky!

Who shall hear of us
in the time to come?
Let him say there was
a burst of fragrance
from black branches.

William Carlos Williams

Love is measured,

not in moments of time,

But in timeless moments.

Barbara Bartocci

TO BE WITH YOU

I want you near
    at the first break of dawn
When flowers are kissed
    by the dew.
I need your love
    like the earth needs the rain,
Like spring needs
    a heaven of blue.

I want your smile
    when the bright noonday sun
Caresses your cheek
    and your hair
As you walk down
    the rose-bordered pathway,
A picture
    of loveliness there.

I want to hear the sweet sound
    of your voice,
To be with you
    wherever you are,
When God gently draws
    the curtains of night
And fastens them shut
    with a star.

Reginald Holmes

ENDURING TREASURES

Love views each day
with eager eyes,
with wonder and surprise,
with fresh delight
in simple pleasures.
    Love dreams its dreams
    and dries its tears,
    and through the busy years
    gathers bright,
    enduring treasures.

Barbara Burrow

This is the miracle that happens every time
to those who really love: the more they give,
the more they possess of that precious
nourishing love from which flowers and
children have their strength and which could
help all human beings if they would take it
without doubting.

Rainer Maria Rilke

MY LOVE FOR YOU

As sure as sunshine after rain,
As peaceful as a country lane,
As warm as fields of summer grain
Is my love for you.
As sentimental as a song,
As steadfast as an oak, as strong,
Growing and deepening all life long
Is my love for you.
And through the many happy years—
Through trials and triumphs,
            smiles and tears—
A wondrous blessing that time endears
Will be my love for you.

Barbara Burrow

WORDS FOR AN AUTUMN HEART

No one told me love was this,
Beyond a dream, beyond a kiss,
No one told me after-Spring
Is sweeter for remembering.
But resting here past heart's midsummer,
Free at last from any rumor
Youth may whisper or imply,
Seeing soundly, eye to eye,
We are as rich as sun's bright gold,
Not quite young, not quite old,
But wise at last to Autumn weather
Blending skillfully together
The bud of Spring and Summer's flower,
That we may wear this little hour
Of sweet content in heart's ripe earth,
And pass it on, for what it's worth!

Gladys McKee

Love is friendship

set to music.

Pollock

HOUR OF NIGHT

We have come home
                and closed the door
After an evening city-bright,
Home to familiar wall and floor.
Let us turn out each light,
Saving one quiet hour more
To know the night.

Draw back the curtain. Let a star,
A hill and pine tree tell us why
The heart-deep satisfactions are
A spot of earth, a square of sky,
A full moon only treetop-far
And you and I.

Esther York Burkholder

A bond of love
        is the surest way
of holding hearts together.

Steven Rustad

COMMUTERS' SPECIAL

All day I function
 happily enough
 in second gear, say,
 with some little part
 idled. A joke is tucked
 inside my heart
 for later sharing;
 any newborn, buff
 kitten, new-blossomed tree,
 cannot be relished fully
 till night, certified
 and embellished
 by love's companionship.

Dusk settles down,
 a half-moon climbs, the cars
 roll in from town,
 incidents rise to mind
 like cream, life quickens,
 the cat perks up,
 the pallid gravy thickens
 and browns, rich odors
 crust a casserole,
 you come through the door.
 And I am whole.

Florence B. Jacobs

HARMONY

Sometimes it seems
    our two hearts beat as one
In perfect time,
Your breath and mine
    are drawn in unison,
And our sighs rhyme.
Because of this, all
    the world's in harmony:
The songs of birds
Are learned from our singing,
    and all poetry
Echoes our words.

Barbara Kunz Loots

LOVE IS A CONSTANT THING

There is no variableness,
        there is no turning,
When Love sets out
        upon its long highroad,
Storms cannot bind it,
        nor the hills deter it;
These cannot keep it
        from its own abode.
Lustily it climbs
        the hills of morning;
Lustily it strides
        the valley loam.
Its feet are swift
        upon the slopes of evening
Taking its
        sure way home.

There is no variableness,
        there is no turning;
The song upon its lips
        remains the same,
Years cannot stifle it,
        nor the dust smother
The song, if love
        be worthy of the name....

Life cannot blind
     its eyes at all, nor dying
Blot out its poignant,
     clear remembering;
Love is a permanent,
     a bright insistence,
Love is
     a constant thing.

Grace Noll Crowell

Love does not consist
     in gazing at each other
but in looking together
     in the same
     direction.

Antoine de Saint-Exupéry

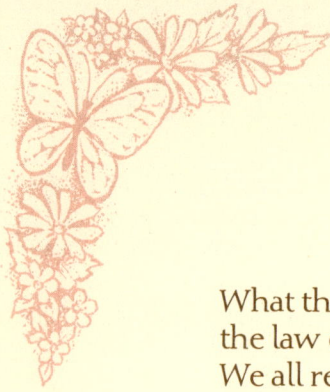

THE LAW OF LOVE

What the law of gravity is to stars and sun,
the law of love is to men and women....
We all retain our sanity by the conviction
that we are needed today and tomorrow,
and by the memory of love that we have
experienced—given or received—which
already has become blood of our blood
and spirit of our spirit.

Joshua Loth Liebman

For I do love you...

as the dew loves the flowers;

as the birds

love the sunshine;

as the wavelets

love the breeze.

Mark Twain

WHERE LOVE HAS WALKED

Something of magic
            clings about a place
Where Love has walked
            in youth's bright ecstasy:
A gateway where a girl's
            young flower face
Was lifted for a first kiss; or a tree
Beneath which lovers
            picnicked once in spring;
A lane where they strolled
            hand in hand; a room
In candlelight where he gave her a ring,
Such places ever after
            wear a bloom.
And we, who go unknowing of their past,
May sense enchantment there,
            we know not why;
May find a wonder and delight to last
Beyond the moment
            or the casual eye.
A brush of stardust
            lingers long around
All places where Love's
            bright dream was found.

Esther York Burkholder

JANUARY LOVE LETTER

I could be merry in a colder climate,
your love to warm me and your arms to hold,
our comradeship without a clock to time it,
our hearth fire whispering, our peace untold.

I could be glad of winter, spreading silence
white as a swan across the frozen hills,
levelling lake and stream in silver balance,
piling huge downy drifts against our sills.

We could outface all storms, were we together,
and there is nothing I would rather do
in all the world, in January weather,
than spend a month, a life, snowed in with you.

Frances Higginson Savage

MOMENT SHARED BY LOVERS

No words are needed
        As we stand
        And watch the sunset glow
        Across the land;
        It is enough to share this moment
        Hand in hand.

Katherine Nelson Davis

MUSIC FOR SPRING

The warm world listens
in this spring of spacious days
and nights, by contrast,
closely wrapped
in rain,
charged with lightning
outside and within
as we begin together
to compose a concert:
songs before unknown
that will transcend
all understanding,
        place and time
except our own.

Charlotte Todd

42

THE BASIC PASSION

Love is the basic passion of man. Every emotion of the heart is reducible to it. Without love we would never become better, for love is the impetus to perfection, the fulfillment of what we have not....

Love is an inclination or a tendency to seek what seems good. The lover seeks union with the good which is loved in order to be perfected by it. The mystery of all love is that it actually precedes every act of choice; one chooses because he loves, he does not love because he chooses. As St. Thomas put it, "All other passions and appetites presuppose love as their first root."

Fulton J. Sheen

Love is something eternal — the aspect may change, but not the essence.

Vincent van Gogh

SONG

You bound strong sandals
on my feet,
You gave me bread and wine,
And sent me
under sun and stars,
For all the world was mine.

Oh, take the sandals
off my feet,
You know not what you do;
For all my world
is in your arms,
My sun and stars are you.

Sara Teasdale

Time deepens love
as summer deepens
the tint of the rose.

Cecil Nelson

MOTIF

All our days
      are a blend of one:
Warm and gold
      with summer sun

That day we stood
      on a sand dune hill
With the lake below us,
      blue and still.

Time holds forever
      within its hand
The frothy waves
      on the cool, wet sand,

The hill, the lake,
      and the widespread skies,
And the kiss that suddenly
      flamed your eyes.

Through the changing pattern
      of our years
The golden thread
      of that day appears.

Kay Wissinger

NEW FOREVER

Some things are new forever:
Morning's long, pink fingers
Reaching up to outline day;
Earth after rain; fresh fallen snow;
The old, old pledges of young love—
And May.

Clara Aiken Speer

BUTTERCUP FIELDS

I remember our first summer,
    Buttercup fields
    And the scent of hay.
I remember evening falling
    And walking hand in hand
    At the close of day.
Sunsets seemed so much more lovely
    Than sunsets
    Ever seemed before,
When you and I would walk together
    In buttercup fields
    In the days of yore.
Somehow, summer never left us,
    We saved its sunshine
    In our hearts
And never knew the chill of winter,
    For we shared the warmth
    That love imparts.
Thanks for all the joys of summer,
    More than that
    What can I say?
Except that always I'll remember
    Buttercup fields
    And the scent of hay.

Robert Wood

from AUTUMN LOVESONG

Unbored,
We have soared
On levels where life's patterns run,
Springtime with blossoms in our eyes,
With the bright wings of butterflies,
And summertime with growth and sun,
A time to shape and mould
     the things undone.
Unbored, we have soared,
Until older, yes, but none too wise,
For we have starlight in our eyes.

Jesse Stuart

Love that knows

    but one season,

has not been seasoned

    properly.

Jean Herrod

Love vanquishes time. To lovers, a moment
can be eternity, eternity can be the tick
of a clock. Across the barriers of time and
the ultimate destiny, love persists, for the
home of the beloved, absent or present,
is always in the mind and heart. Absence
does not diminish love.

Mary Parrish

Is it so small a thing
        To have enjoyed the sun,
To have lived light
        in the spring,
To have loved,
        To have thought,
To have done?

Matthew Arnold

AT NIGHTFALL

I need so much
    the quiet of your love,
  After the day's loud strife;
I need your calm
    all other things above,
  After the stress of life.

I crave the haven
    that in your dear heart lies,
  After all toil is done;
I need the starshine
    of your heavenly eyes,
  After the day's great sun.

Charles Hanson Towne

NOW AND THEN

How filled with seductive charms
Love in young fashion is.
But be glad that even old arms
Embrace love, longer than beauty,
Longer than passion is.

Charlotte Todd

FOR YOU, MY LOVE

You're as lovely
as a June afternoon
when the sky
is a flawless blue,
When the breeze
is caressingly soft,
And my world is a blend
of sky
and earth
and you.

Cecil Long

THE PROMISE OF LOVE

The promise of love
 holds a magic for two,
a bright and beautiful
 dream coming true.
The promise of love
 means a new life unfolding,
a sharing, a caring,
 a having and holding.
It's a vow that brings two hearts
 together as one,
together in everything —
 sorrows and fun.
It's a promise to master
 the fine art of giving,
an adventure for two
 in the joy that is living.
The promise of love
 shines with hope like a star,
it says, "I'll be there
 wherever you are."
The promise of love is renewed
 with each day,
a brand-new beginning's
 a sunrise away....

It is looking together
　　　　through the world's windowpane
　　at the passing of seasons,
　　　　at sunshine and rain.
Love's a promise that glows
　　　　with perpetual youth,
　　a cup overflowing
　　　　with kindness and truth.
It's a pathway of happiness
　　　　down through the years
　　lined with flowers of laughter
　　　　and dewdrops of tears.
It's a song of delight
　　　　and a sonnet of glory,
　　a daily unfolding of love's
　　　　own sweet story
as the plans that you've made,
all the things you've
　　　　dreamed of,
all your hopes are fulfilled
　　　　by the promise of Love.

Julia Summers

O love, my world is you!

Christina Rossetti

WHERE LOVE IS FOUND

Love is found in the midnight sky
And in the moonlight's glow.
Love is found in the robin's song
And where rippling rivers flow.
Love is found on a summer's day;
It's where the sunrise starts.
And love can be found wherever
Two people give their hearts.

Benjamin Whitley

What's the earth

With all its art,

verse, music, worth—

Compared with love, found,

gained and kept?

Robert Browning

BUT FOR LOVE

But for love
    I'd never know
    the happiness of sharing...
But for love
I'd never know
the tenderness of caring...
But for love
I'd never know
the joy of dreams come true...
But for love
I'd never know
the miracle of you.

George Webster Douglas

IMPERFECTION

I can't remember the exact moment
I noticed he wasn't perfect. I just know
I didn't feel shaken or even very worried.
We are stronger than that—or is it our
love that can bend like a sapling and still
grow straight and tall.

Tina Hacker

MEMORY PICTURES

A memory
is a photograph
taken by the heart
To make
a special moment
last forever…
And of all
the memory-pictures
that happy times have brought,
My favorites
are the ones
we've made together.

John Grey

I LOVE YOU

I love you for that certain smile
   That cheers me when I'm blue,
   I love you for your tender kiss
   That warms me through and through.
   I love you for your gentle hand,
   Your understanding touch,
   Your eyes that somehow seem to say,
"I love you very much."
   I love you for your faith in me,
   For your sweet patient ways,
   For the many thoughtful things you do
   So often without praise.
   I love you, Dear, for all these things
   And for a million others, too,
   But most of all — for what I am
   Whenever I'm with you!

Mary Volk

Set in Diotima, a calligraphic roman
designed in 1954 by Gudrun Zapf von Hesse.
Printed on Hallmark Ivory Vellux.
Designed by Rainer K. Koenig.